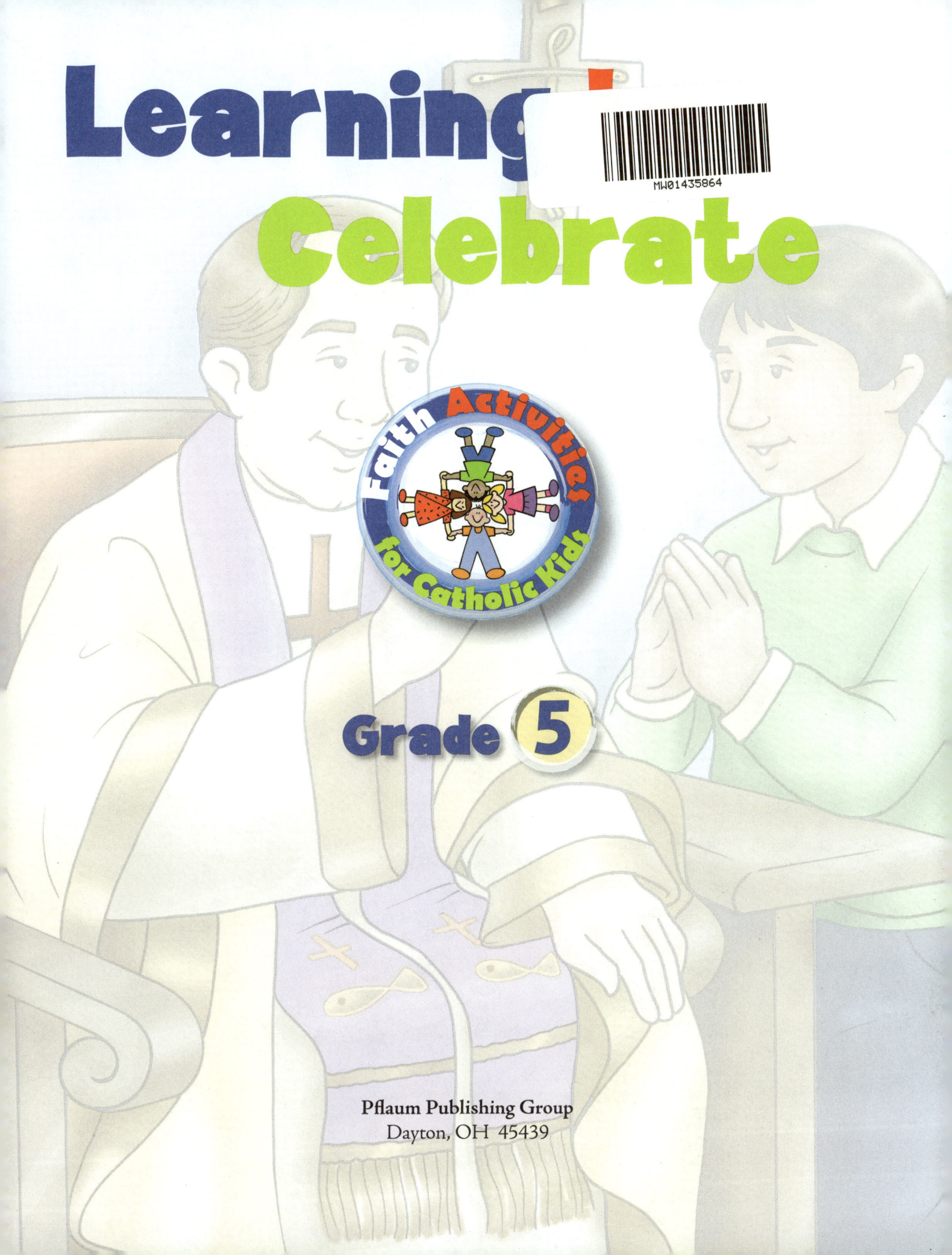

Learning to Celebrate

Faith Activities for Catholic Kids

Grade 5

Pflaum Publishing Group
Dayton, OH 45439

Faith Activities

Learning to Celebrate
Faith Activities for Catholic Kids
Grade 5

Content and design by Victory Productions, Worcester, MA 01609
General Editors: Karen Cannizzo and Cullen Schippe

© 2005 Pflaum Publishing Group, Dayton, OH 45439 (800-543-4383) pflaum.com Published in Milwaukee, WI 53051 All rights reserved. No part of this text may be reproduced in any way or for any use without the written permission of the publisher.

Third Printing: 2009

Nihil obstat: Reverend Monsignor John F. Murphy, *censor librorum*,
May 24, 2005

Imprimatur: † Most Reverend Timothy M. Dolan, Archbishop of Milwaukee,
June 2, 2005

Scripture quotations contained herein are from the *New Revised Standard Version Bible*: Catholic Edition, © 1993 and 1989 by the Division of Christian Education of the National Council of the Churches of Christ in the United States of America. Used by permission. All rights reserved.

ISBN 978-1-933178-19-6

for Catholic Kids

Contents

I Believe

A People Detective	4
A Holy Mystery	5
Signs of God	6
Jesus Is a Sign of God's Grace	7
The Holy Spirit	8
The Marks of the Church	9
Who Is the Church?	10
The Communion of Saints	11

I Celebrate

God Is Here	12
Sealed with the Holy Spirit	13
One with Jesus	14
A Sacrament of Forgiveness	15
God Gives Strength	16
Showing God's Love	17
Serving the Church	18

I Follow Jesus

Mary, Our Role Model	19
Yes Is a Powerful Word	20
Making Moral Choices	21
All of a Kind	22
God Gives Gifts	23
The Choices You Make	24
The Unforgiving Servant	25

I Pray

Finding God	26
I Believe	27
The Prayer of the Church	28
Why Do We Pray?	29
My Response to God's Love	30
The Church Responds to God's Love	31
A Year in the Church	32

I Believe

A People Detective

Life is filled with many signs. All signs are discovered through your senses. Many signs are given in words or drawings. These signs, such as traffic signs, usually give information.

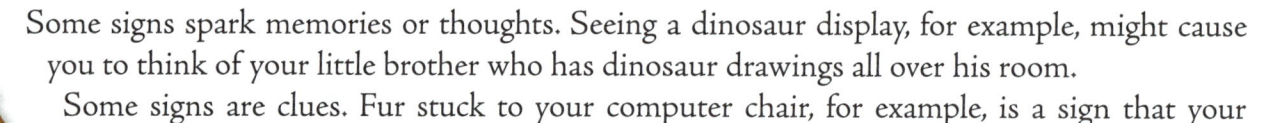

Some signs spark memories or thoughts. Seeing a dinosaur display, for example, might cause you to think of your little brother who has dinosaur drawings all over his room.

Some signs are clues. Fur stuck to your computer chair, for example, is a sign that your cat uses the chair as a bed.

Draw a sign that gives information about your bedroom.

Pretend you've lost a pet. Draw a sign that would remind you of your pet.

On the Look-Out

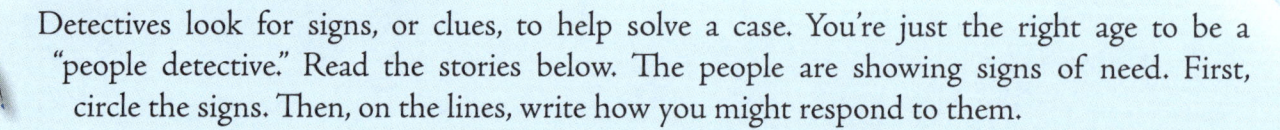

Detectives look for signs, or clues, to help solve a case. You're just the right age to be a "people detective." Read the stories below. The people are showing signs of need. First, circle the signs. Then, on the lines, write how you might respond to them.

1. Bryan is usually picked last for a team. By then, his head droops and his feet drag.

   _____

2. Your little sister's eyes are wet with tears. She has a spelling test tomorrow. She got a "D" on the last test.

   _____

3. Mom unloads the groceries, plops onto a chair, and sighs. "Whew! It's been a long day," she says.

   _____

Signs of God

A Holy Mystery

The letters *tri-* as a prefix in a word give a clue about the word's meaning. *Tri-* means "three."

How many wheels does a tricycle have? _____

How many horns did a triceratops have? _____

Catholics believe in the Holy Trinity. The letters *tri* give a clue to the belief. The Holy Trinity is the belief in one God in three persons—God the Father, God the Son, and God the Holy Spirit.

Signs That Teach

The Church uses pictures and objects as signs to help people understand the mystery of the Holy Trinity.

Saint Patrick used the three-leafed shamrock that grows in Ireland to teach about the mystery of the Holy Trinity. Each part of the shamrock is a sign of a belief.

The single stem stands for the belief: There is one God.
The shamrock leaves stand for the beliefs:
1. The one God is three persons.
2. Each of the three persons is God.
3. Each of the three persons reveal God in a different way.

Look at the three linked circles. What other shape do you see?

Explain to a friend or family member how this drawing illustrates the doctrine of the Holy Trinity. Next time you're in church, look around for signs and pictures that represent the Holy Trinity.

Draw your own sign or symbol for the Holy Trinity.

And that's a fact...

If we can't see or hear or touch God, why do we say that God is three persons? The Trinity is a mystery. That means we cannot completely understand that God is three persons. But Jesus revealed the Trinity to us. He told his disciples to baptize "in the name of Father and of the Son and of the Holy Spirit." (Matthew 28:19)

I Believe

Signs of God

God the Creator blesses us with signs of his presence. All of creation is God's good gift to us and reminds us that God is always with us.

Make a Mobile

All God created is good, including you. You share in God's goodness when you practice stewardship, which is a respectful response to all of creation. Make a mobile that shows how you are connected to God's good gifts.

1. Using poster board, cut out a circle, about 10 inches around.
2. Read the four verses from Genesis, the first book in the Bible.
3. Cover both sides of the circle with pictures of God's creation.
4. Now make the holes. Punch one in the circle's center and punch four in different places to balance what you'll hang.
5. Using yarn, tie and hang the four verses, one at a time, to the four holes. Think about each verse and how you, a fifth grader, can respect the creation mentioned in it. Draw or write your response on a small piece of drawing paper. Be as specific as you can be.
6. Now hang your response from the bottom of each verse. Cut a long piece of yarn to tie to the center hole. That's the piece you'll use to hang the mobile.

You'll need:
- scissors
- poster board of any color
- hole punch
- yarn
- glue
- magazines with lots of pictures
- drawing paper
- markers, crayons, or colored pencils

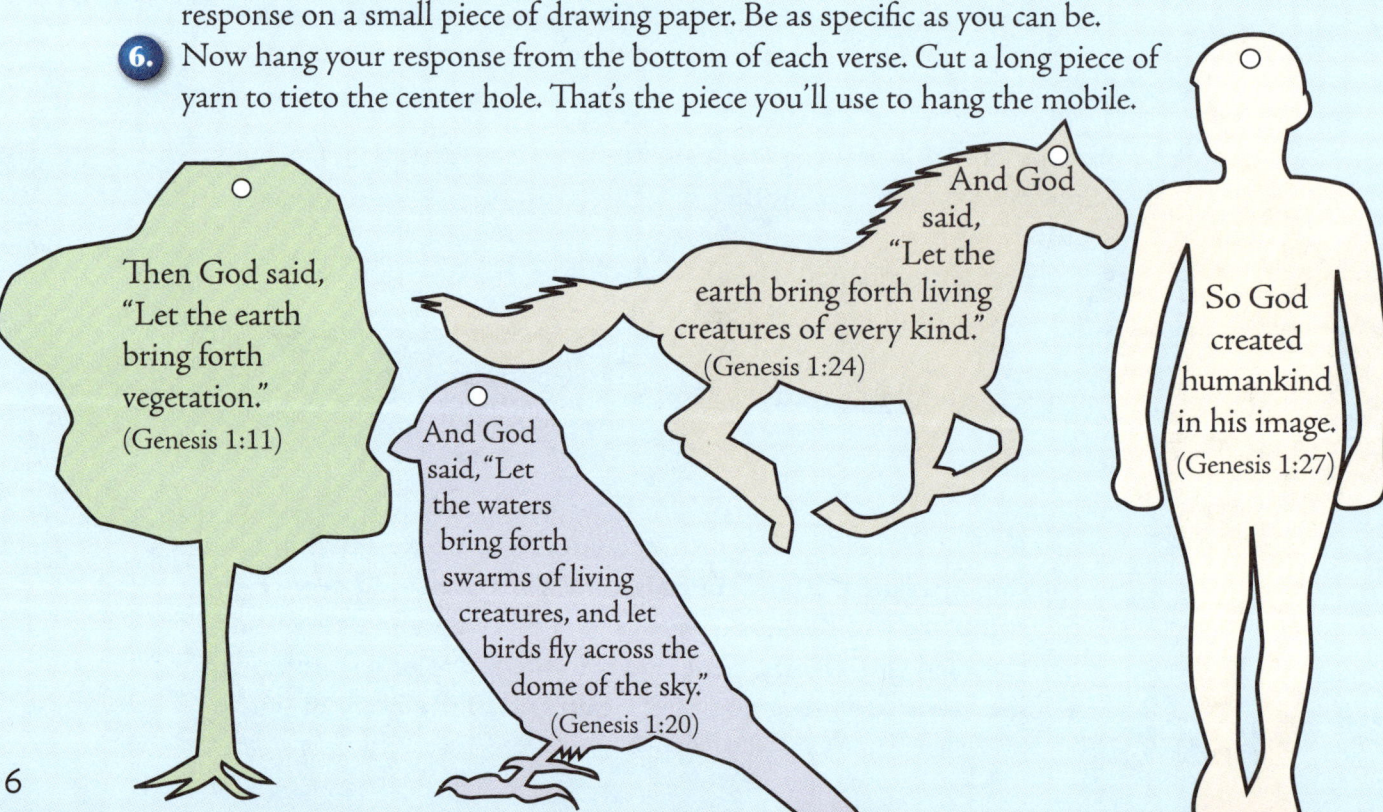

Then God said, "Let the earth bring forth vegetation." (Genesis 1:11)

And God said, "Let the waters bring forth swarms of living creatures, and let birds fly across the dome of the sky." (Genesis 1:20)

And God said, "Let the earth bring forth living creatures of every kind." (Genesis 1:24)

So God created humankind in his image. (Genesis 1:27)

Signs of God

Jesus Is a Sign of God's Grace

Your actions and words are signs that tell about you.

If you're kicking a chair and scowling, you're probably feeling _____.

If you tell Emily you like the way she plays the piano, you're probably being _____.

> **Jesus is God the Son, the Second Person of the Holy Trinity. Jesus' whole life was a sign of God's grace. That's another way of saying that everything Jesus said and did showed God's life in him.**

Read about Jesus and imagine yourself as a person in the story. On each line, write how Jesus' actions and words tell you about God.

Jesus gently touched two blind men's eyes.
Jesus asked the men to trust in him.
The men did and they could see. (See Matthew 9:28-30.)

_____

A sinful woman came to Jesus and asked for forgiveness. The other people told Jesus to ignore her. Jesus said to the woman, "Your sins are forgiven." (See Luke 7:36-50.)

_____

A lawyer asked Jesus, "What is the greatest commandment?" Jesus said, "Love God above all and love your neighbor as yourself." (See Matthew 22:36-39.)

_____

I'm a Sign, Too

In your everyday life, you can be a sign of God's grace. Play this game to figure out how.

- Choose one of the 3 action words, or let a partner choose one for you.

  Love   Heal   Forgive

- Close your eyes and twirl a finger over the circle. Let your finger land on a place.

- Tell a specific way you can love, heal, or forgive the people in that place.

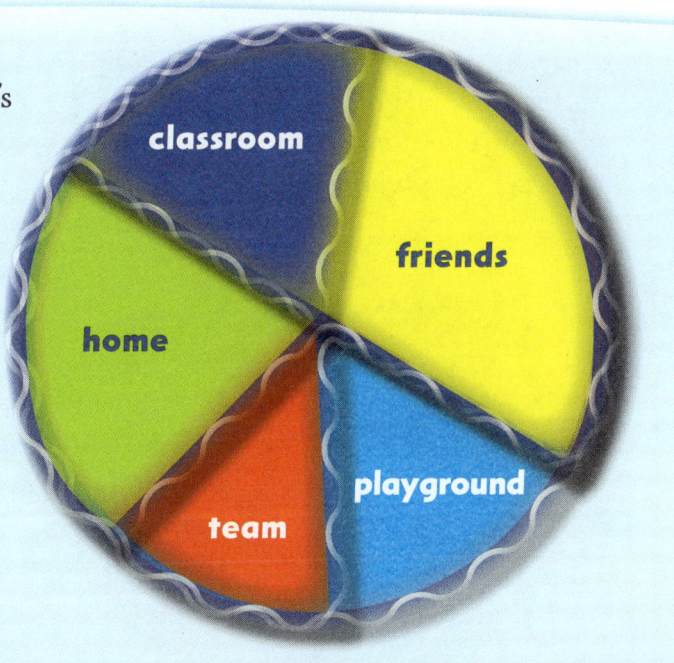

7

I Believe

The Holy Spirit

Think of a time when you felt full of spirit and excitement, when you felt strong and able to do something difficult.

Every day most people make choices between right and wrong. The Holy Spirit is the power, the strength, and the grace that helps people make good choices. That's why another name for the Holy Spirit is Giver of Life. The Holy Spirit is an unseen power that is always with you.

Take a Closer Look

The Spirit's presence in your life is a constant sign of God's love for you.

Each clue below refers to a letter of the alphabet. Write the letter on the line. The letters will read vertically and spell a name that Jesus used to describe the Holy Spirit.

1. I'm in SPACE, but not in SPICE.
2. I'm in GRAND, but not in GRAIN.
3. I'm in LIVER, but not in LINER.
4. I'm in SCORE, but not in CARES.
5. I'm in RELICS, but not in PLIERS.
6. I'm in AMPLE, but not in PLUME.
7. I'm in MONSTER, but not in SERMON.
8. I'm in RIDGE, but not in GRIND.

Jesus called the Holy Spirit an _____. By using that name, Jesus was describing the role of the Holy Spirit. The Holy Spirit is your support, helping you stay close to God.

And that's a fact...

Fire and wind are two symbols that show us the power of the Holy Spirit. You know the power of wind. Think of the cold winter wind that you can feel through your coat. Think of the wind that moves a sailboat. Fire produces great energy in heat and light. Read Acts 2:1-4, to learn how the power of the Holy Spirit came to the apostles on Pentecost.

Signs of God

The Marks of the Church

How do you know what a person is like? You can see the qualities, or characteristics, of a person in his or her actions. When you see a person being courteous to others, these actions tell you about the person. Courtesy is a characteristic of a caring person.

Write the name of someone you know who is a caring person. What are some characteristics that show this person's care for others? Write the characteristics here.

_____

_____

_____

The Church has four important characteristics that tell us what the Church is like. These characteristics are called the marks of the Church. These marks are signs of the presence of the Holy Spirit in the Church.

Make a Mark

Find the words that complete the sentences about the marks of the Church. Write the words in the blanks. Then, under each mark in the left column, make up a sign of the Holy Spirit. Use words or pictures.

| Jesus | news | join | justice | unites | Apostles |

one		The Holy Spirit _____ God's people. They share one faith in God and one Baptism in Jesus.
holy		The Holy Spirit helps God's people to live like Jesus. They show love, _____, and mercy.
catholic		The word *catholic* means "open to all." The Holy Spirit invites everyone to _____ the Church and follow _____.
apostolic		The Holy Spirit guides the Church to teach the good _____ passed on by the _____.

9

I Believe

Who Is the Church?

Traditional Native American names tell something about what is being named. The Lakota tribe, for example, calls the Creator *Wakan Tanka* (Wah-kon Ton'kah), which means "Grandfather — Great Spirit."

Use a phrase to make up a name for these boys and girls.
Example: a girl who runs fast   Swift as a Deer

a boy with bright red hair   _____

a girl who makes people smile   _____

a boy who always shares   _____

Names Are Signs

The Bible uses different names for the Church. Each name tells something about the followers of Jesus who are the Catholic Church. Each name shows that the Church is a sign of God's union with us.

The Scripture passages on the left tell us about the Church. On the right are names we use for the Church. Draw lines to connect the matches.

"Once you were not a people, but now you are God's people."
(1 Peter 2:10)

"Do you not know that you are God's temple and that God's Spirit dwells in you?"
(1 Corinthians 3:16)

"For in the one Spirit we were all baptized into one body."
(1 Corinthians 12:13)

The name *Temple of the Holy Spirit* describes the mission of the Church. The Church is like a temple, or sacred building. Its people are the stones, and Jesus is the cornerstone.

The name *Body of Christ* tells about the Church's relationship with Jesus. The Church is one Body of people who follow Jesus, the head of the Church.

The name *People of God* says that baptized Catholics who worship together belong to God the Father. They love as Jesus loves. They are filled with the Holy Spirit.

Signs of God

The Communion of Saints

Have you been told about ways you resemble your relatives? Perhaps you walk like your great-grandfather, or you're generous like your grandmother. You're physically connected to generations of your ancestors, living and dead.

Catholics believe that the Family of God is one family of people, living and dead. They are united by Baptism. This family is called the communion of saints.

Living Like Jesus

Saints are people whose lives shine with the love of God. Artists like to show the goodness of saints by painting a halo of light around or above their heads. Look at the three halos below that stand for the communion of saints.

- In the first halo, name a saint of the Church. On the lines below, tell a way that person led a holy life.
- In the second halo, name a person you know or have heard about who is holy and lives like Jesus. Tell something good the person does.
- In the third halo, write your name. On the lines below, tell about a goal you have to live a holy life.

And that's a fact...

The Church declares some holy people who have died to be saints. These are people who have led such good lives that the Church decides they are enjoying the full presence of God. The Church studies a person's life very carefully before making this decision. Then the person is "canonized". That means his or her name is added to the *canon*, the list of the Church's saints. These holy people are models for us to follow.

I Celebrate

God Is Here

Signs can reveal more than you can know through your senses.

Sam let the door slam shut. He flung his backpack on the kitchen counter. Sam noticed the teakettle on the stove and a tea bag nearby, ready for dunking. "Mom must have gotten home early," thought Sam.

Sam didn't see his mom, but he knew she was there. Circle signs in the story that showed Sam's mom was home.

> We can't see God, but Jesus gives signs of God's presence. The Church celebrates seven signs as sacraments. Each sacrament uses ordinary objects we know through our senses. And each sacrament reveals more to us. In the sacraments, the invisible God speaks, heals, loves, nourishes, and strengthens. That's why sacraments are called celebrations.

KNOWING GOD

Jesus' baptism marked the beginning of his public ministry, when he began preaching the word of God. The Church calls Baptism, Confirmation, and Eucharist the sacraments of initiation, for they are beginnings, too. Find out how Baptism initiated you into Christian life. Decode the words using the letter that appears before it in the alphabet.

In Baptism…

you join the __ __ __ __ __ __ __ __ __ __ __ __ __ __, the Church,
            C P E Z   P G   D I S J T U

you promise to __ __ __ __ __ __ __ __ __ __ __,
               G P M M P X   K F T V T

you share in the __ __ __ __ of the __ __ __ __ __ __ __ __ __ __ __ __,
                  M J G F   I P M Z   U S J O J U Z

God forgives your __ __ __ __.
                   T J O T

And that's a fact...

Anyone can baptize an unbaptized person who is in danger of dying. Ordinary water is poured on the person's head while these words are said: "I baptize you in the name of the Father, and of the Son, and of the Holy Spirit."

The Sacraments

Sealed with the Holy Spirit

Kings and queens sealed important documents with wax and an individual mark of identification. Use your initals to create your own mark of identification in the box.

Baptism initiated you into the Church and made you a Christian. Confirmation is the sacrament of initiation that seals, or confirms, your role to live a Christian life. In Confirmation, a bishop dips his finger into holy oil, lays his hand on your head, and marks your forehead with the sign of the cross. The sweet-smelling, shiny oil is a visible sign of the presence of the Holy Spirit.

Acting with Courage

In Baptism and in Confirmation, you receive the gifts of the Holy Spirit that help you live a Christian life. One of the gifts is the courage to do what is right. Imagine that these glasses help you use the Holy Spirit's gift of courage. To begin, choose any person from the left lens and any action from the right. On the lines, write a specific act of Christian courage. Then, decorate the glasses any way you wish.

eighth grader
friend
neighbor

bullies
makes fun of others
says it's okay to steal
small items

13

I Celebrate

One with Jesus

When you chomp on an apple, do you ever imagine it feeding your hair or your nails? Every part of your body is fed and nourished by the food you eat. On the menu, list some foods that you feel are important for you to grow strong and healthy.

Menu

Discover the words of Jesus in which he describes himself as food. Write in the missing vowels.

"__ __m th__ l__v__ng br__ __d th__t c__m__ d__wn fr__m h__ __v__n. Wh__ __v__r __ __ts th__s br__ __d w__ll l__v__ f__r__v__r." (John 6:51)

The Bread of Life

The sacrament of the Eucharist completes your Christian initiation. In Baptism you are born into a new life in Jesus. In Confirmation you are strengthened to live a Christian life. In Eucharist you are nourished with Jesus, the bread of eternal life.

The sacrament of the Eucharist is the Mass and Holy Communion. Jesus is present in the gathered community, in the Word of God, and in the breaking of the bread. When you eat the bread and drink the cup, you are one with, or in communion with, Jesus. At the end of Mass, you are sent to live like Jesus.

And that's a fact...

If you had lived 100 years ago, you wouldn't be old enough to receive Holy Communion. At that time, young people couldn't receive the Eucharist until they were twelve years of age or older. In 1910, Pius X changed Church rules so that children could receive Holy Communion when they were old enough to know and love Jesus. St. Pius was known for encouraging people to receive Communion frequently, even daily.

The Sacraments

A Sacrament of Forgiveness

All friendships, including your friendship with Jesus, rely on forgiveness. Friends admit when they've done wrong. They say they're sorry, ask for forgiveness, and promise not to do the same thing again.

> Jesus shows his loving forgiveness in the sacrament of Reconciliation. Jesus is present in the sacrament. The priest offers you forgiveness in Jesus' name. Jesus, through the actions of the priest, takes away your sins and helps you avoid sin in the future.

Ouch! That Hurts!

Take some quiet time to think about forgiveness in your life. Read the hurtful actions listed here. If you find the action hard to forgive, check the circle next to it. If you find it difficult to say "I'm sorry" for the action, check the circle next to it.

Hard to Forgive
- I'm made fun of.
- I'm lied to.
- My secret is told.
- Someone hits me on purpose.
- My stuff is stolen.
- I'm talked back to.

Hard to Say I'm Sorry
- I make fun of someone.
- I lie.
- I tell a secret.
- I hit someone on purpose.
- I steal.
- I talk back.

How do I feel when I'm forgiven?
_____
_____

How can I be a good forgiver?
_____
_____

Why is forgiveness important?
_____

And that's a fact...

Before the year 700, people didn't confess their sins privately. Sinners put on scratchy sack clothing and put ashes on their heads. They appeared in public for all to see.

15

I Celebrate

God Gives Strength

Draw hearts around the words that you associate with healing.

cough syrup   aspirin   hugs   smiles

doctor   friend   get-well card   operation

When people get sick their bodies <u>and</u> their spirits need healing. The ill depend on a doctor's knowledge and on people's kindness to help them get better.

> God brings his loving presence in a sacramental way to those who are very ill, elderly, or dying. The sacrament of Anointing of the Sick offers them God's healing and comfort. Their pain and illness might not go away. But the sacrament, through God's grace, brings healing of the body and the spirit. The ill know and feel God's love. They have a sense of peace.

I Bring Comfort

God's presence is known through the sacrament of Anointing and also through you.

You make God's presence known when you show love and care for people who face challenges. It's awful to be sick or injured. Look at the illustration. Draw people and things that would bring God's healing touch to this boy.

The Sacraments

Showing God's Love

Write a promise you once made.

_____
_____
_____

> For Christians, some promises are made with God. In a church, before witnesses, a bride and groom make sacred promises, or vows. The couple promise God and each other to be faithful and loving. The sacrament of Marriage happens when they make the promises. As a symbol of their vows, the couple often exchanges rings.

When Catholics Marry

Through the love they show each other, the husband and wife are a sign of God's love.

Use the clues to complete this crossword puzzle about the Sacrament of Marriage.

ACROSS
5 Marriage is one of the seven _____.
7 The ministers of Marriage are the _____.

DOWN
1 Sacred promises
2 Where Catholics marry
3 The couple promises to be _____.
4 A sign of faithfulness
6 The couple is a _____ of God's love.

17

I Celebrate

Serving the Church

Some men are ordained, or given a priestly role in the Church. They receive the sacrament of Holy Orders. This sacrament gives them the grace and responsibility to serve God's people.

Signs of Service

Ordained ministers may serve in three different roles, or orders. In the sacrament of Holy Orders, each man is given signs of the work he will do. Solve the puzzles to discover the signs.

Deacon

Because he preaches, a deacon is given a

Book of the G O S + [poles] – O ; Switch L and E = __ __ __ __ __ __ .

Because a deacon may assist at Mass, he is given a

S T + [stole] – H = __ __ __ __ __ .

Priest

Because he celebrates the Eucharist, a priest is given a

[chin] + 10 – T = __ __ __ __ __ that holds the hosts for Mass.

A priest also receives a

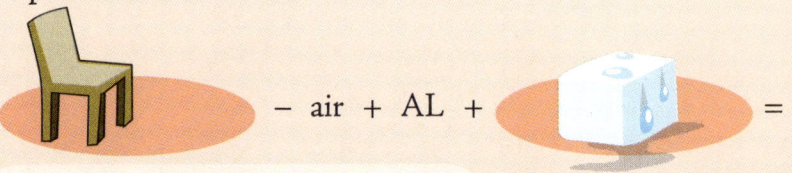

[chair] – air + AL + [ice] = __ __ __ __ __ __ __ that holds the wine for Mass.

Bishop

Because a bishop leads all the people of a diocese, he is given a shepherd's staff, or

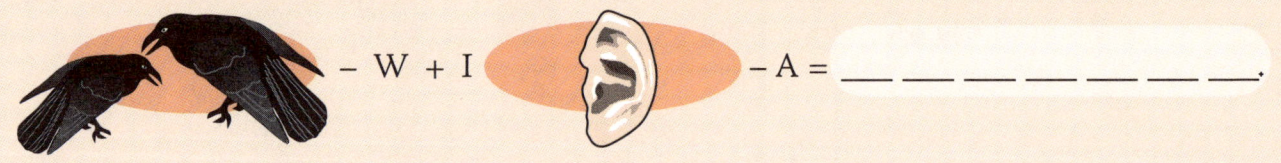

[crows] – W + I + [ear] – A = __ __ __ __ __ __ __ __ .

As a sign of his leadership, a bishop is given a tall hat called a

M + I + [tear] – A = __ __ __ __ __ .

18

I Follow Jesus

Mary, Our Role Model

The Hail Mary describes Mary, the mother of God, as "full of grace." Those three words tell us a lot about Mary. During her whole life, Mary said yes to God and did as he asked. Mary's choices were signs of God's goodness within her.

If you met Mary, what do you think you would like most about her?

_____

Be Like Mary

The Gospels tell many stories about Mary. Four are retold here. Read each story and then read the contemporary story that goes with it. For each of today's stories, write a way that the person can act like Mary.

The angel told Mary that she would be the mother of God. The angel's words confused Mary. But Mary trusted in God's goodness and said she would do what God asked of her.

Charley had plans for Saturday. He was meeting his friends at the park for baseball practice. But on Friday evening, Charley's mom said, "Charley, I really need you to watch Meghan tomorrow."

Charley can _____.

The angel said that Mary's cousin, Elizabeth, was going to have a baby. Mary knew that Elizabeth needed help, so Mary made the long trip to Elizabeth's house. Mary stayed and helped until the baby was born.

Every Saturday morning Rosa plops down in front of the television. She knows it's cleaning day at her house, but she waits until her mom asks for her help.

Rosa can _____.

Mary and Joseph brought up Jesus in their Jewish faith. They prayed with him. They helped him study the Word of God. As a family, they participated in special religious ceremonies.

Ashley's family is getting ready for Mass. As usual, Ashley's little brother is putting up a fuss. What can Ashley do?

Ashley can _____
_____.

Mary and Jesus were at a wedding celebration. Everyone was having a good time. When Mary noticed that the wine was almost all gone, she talked to Jesus. She knew that Jesus, as God's Son, would help.

Liam has a tough decision to make. He wishes it would just go away. How can Liam get help with his tough decision?

Liam can _____
_____.

19

I Follow Jesus

Yes Is a Powerful Word

Want pizza for lunch? Never any homework? Seven hours of play? And art class every day? Y–E–S spells yes!

Write some questions to which you would always say yes.

_____

_____

_____

> Every day you have opportunities to say yes to God. When you show you care about others, you say yes. When you respect yourself, you say yes. When you accept people who are different from you, you say yes. All of your everyday yeses show your love for God.

Advice Cookies

A bakery experimented with a new batch of cookies made especially for fifth graders. Tucked inside each cookie is a message of advice. Complete the messages below. Tell how a fifth grader can say yes to God.

Before you fall asleep, you can _____

When your mom is tired, you can _____

When your sister cries, you can _____

If you lie to stay out of trouble, you can _____

When you're teased, you can _____

If you're tempted to steal, you can _____

Good Choices

Making Moral Choices

Some choices you make are fun or interesting, but not very important. Circle your picks for each category.

1. chocolate chip
   peanut butter
   sugar cookies

2. baseball
   basketball
   soccer

3. math
   reading
   art

> Sometimes you have to choose between right and wrong. These decisions are called moral choices, and they have consequences. If you lie to a friend, your friend will no longer be able to trust you. Your lie hurts your friendship. Because you feel badly about what you've done, lying hurts you, too. Lying hurts your relationship with God, which is built on your promise to be a good person.

Young children make choices that keep them out of trouble. But you're at just the right age to make a choice because it's the right thing to do.

Facing Consequences

Read each of the following decisions. In the blank, write a possible consequence of the choice that was made.

When your dad's not looking, you punch your brother.
_____

Everyone else teases the new fifth grader, so you do, too.
_____

You lie and say you can't find your homework.
_____

You listen to your teacher explain the lesson.
_____

You tell the truth and say you didn't do your homework.
_____

And that's a fact...

A virtue is an example of doing good in order to grow in love for God. God gifts people with three virtues known as faith, hope, and love. Look around your church for the symbols of these virtues. Hint: Faith is often shown with a cross, hope with an anchor, and love with a heart.

I Follow Jesus

All of a Kind

Pope John Paul II called the people of the world a family. No matter what they look like, what they own, or what language they speak, children have much in common. Draw a star next to what is true about children all over the world.

like to play	need love	need clothes
need food	like jokes	like animals

Some people judge others by the color of their skin, but skin color is just a way that bodies adjust to climate. Skin colors have changed over long periods of time. People who have lived in hot climates developed darker skin tones. The darker colors help protect their bodies from harmful rays of the sun. People in climates where there is much less sun have much lighter skin colors.

Make a Friendship Bracelet

God wants all people to be treated with respect. Make a friendship bracelet as a reminder that all people can be friends. As you work, decide who will receive your bracelet.

1. Use four different colors of embroidery thread, each 24 inches long. If you wish, use colors that are similar to people's skin tones. Hold all four threads and make an overhand knot 8 inches from one end of the threads. Tie the knot to the back of a chair.

2. Put the four colors side by side. Starting with the color on the left, think of each color as a letter of the alphabet—A, B, C, D.

3. Hold A and B in your two hands. Wrap A over and under B, pulling A through the loop with your right hand. Hold B tightly with your left hand and pull up with A. You've made a knot! Repeat the wrapping and make a second knot with thread A over B.

4. Just keep on knotting! Let go of B. Make two knots with A over C. Then make two knots with A over D. You now have used A to make two knots with each of the other three pieces of thread. You probably can guess what comes next.

5. Go on to the second row. Make two knots with B over C. Then knot B over D twice and B over A twice.

6. Continue in the same way with C, beginning with C over D. Finally, use D to go over A, B, and C.

7. When you think the bracelet is long enough to wear, leave some thread to tie the bracelet into a circle. Cut off any excess thread.

Good Choices

God Gives Gifts

The world is a sign of God's presence and goodness.

> "In his hand is the life of every living thing and the breath of every human being." (Job 12:10)

An African-American spiritual celebrates God as the Creator. Sing, clap, and sway to this song:

"He's got the whole world in his hands,
He's got the whole world in his hands,
He's got the whole wide world in his hands,
He's got the whole world in his hands."

Now sing the song again. This time, replace the words "the whole world" with "you and me friend."

Be a Song Writer

A good way to show appreciation for a gift is to treat it with care. Showing respect for yourself and others is a sign of your thankfulness to God.

Make up another verse to "He's Got the Whole World in His Hands" that tells about people God created. For example, you might want to sing, "He's got me and my family in his hands." On a sheet of drawing paper, write the lyrics you made up.

In the box below, draw a way to show respect to those you sing about. How can you show respect to yourself? to your family?

23

I Follow Jesus

The Choices You Make

Some moral choices you make can affect people you love.
If you hit your brother, you hurt your mom, too. Why do you suppose that is?
When you willingly share your computer with your brother, you make your dad happy, too. Why do you suppose that is?

Look at the drawing.
What do you think it means?
Fill in the blank.
When I serve others, I serve _____.

Serve God
Serve Others

The actions and words you direct toward others affect your relationship with God. When you love others, you love God. You help your relationship with God grow.

Linked to God

Show how your choices affect your relationship with God and others. You will need scissors, colored paper, a stapler, and a marker or pen.

Cut four links out of colored paper. On one link write: Serve God.
Write an action of service on each of the other three links. Use the links on this page as samples. Now make a chain of the four links. Staple two links together. Then, add the Serve God link. Complete the chain with the remaining links. Hang your chain where you will see it often.

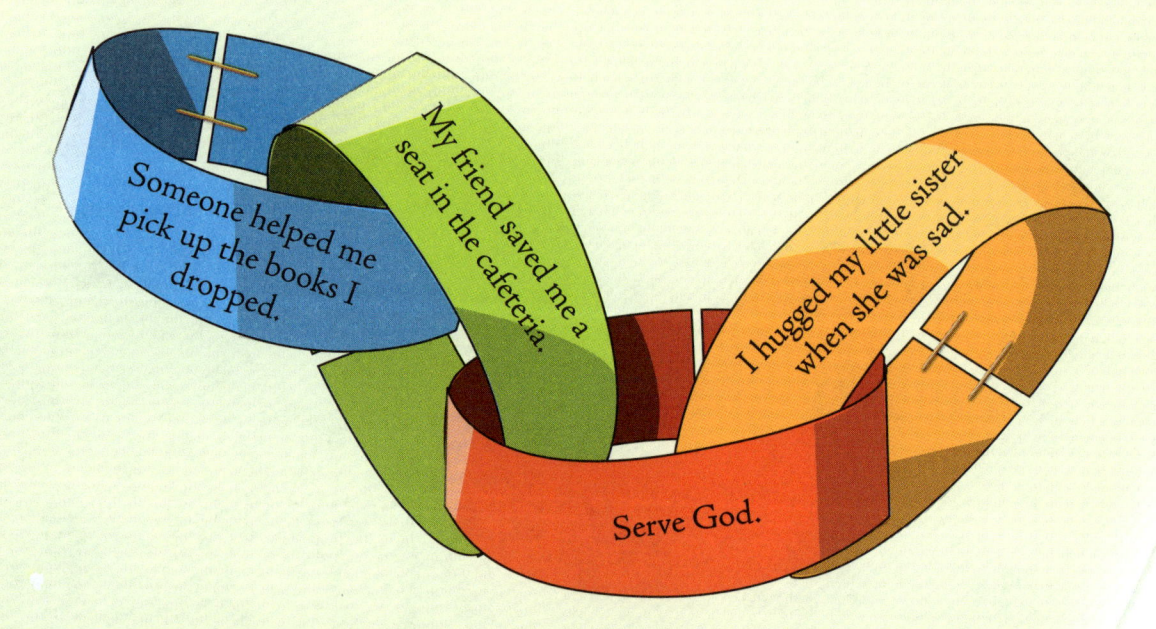

- Someone helped me pick up the books I dropped.
- My friend saved me a seat in the cafeteria.
- I hugged my little sister when she was sad.
- Serve God.

Good Choices

The Unforgiving Servant

Jesus was a storyteller. Some of his stories are called parables because they contain a message for people to figure out. Read this shortened version of one of Jesus' parables.

1. You owe me a lot of money. I'm going to sell you and your family.

2. Have patience with me, and I will pay you everything.

3. I feel sorry for you. You do not have to pay me.

4. Pay **me** what you owe!

Have patience with me, and I will pay you.

5. No! You're off to jail!

6. You wicked servant! I forgave you, yet you didn't show mercy to others. You will be punished!

What is Jesus teaching about forgiveness in his parable? Circle the correct answers.

1. The king in the story is really

    God   everyone   King Henry

2. The servant in the story is really anyone

    who works   who sins   who forgives

3. God forgives and shows sinners

    revenge   mercy   meanness

4. Like the king, we should

    rarely forgive   be forgiving and merciful   forgive people who owe us money

5. Like the king, we should forgive

    only people we like   everyone, even those we don't like   only people who owe us money

I Pray

Finding God

Think about two ways you can reach your friend if you need to talk.

1. _____
2. _____

Is it possible to have a friendship with someone you don't talk to or write to? Friendships depend on communication. Friends need to get to know and understand one another. Your friendship with God also depends on communication. Even though you can't see or hear God, you know signs of his presence. Your prayers are signs of your friendship with God.

Tic-Tac-Talk

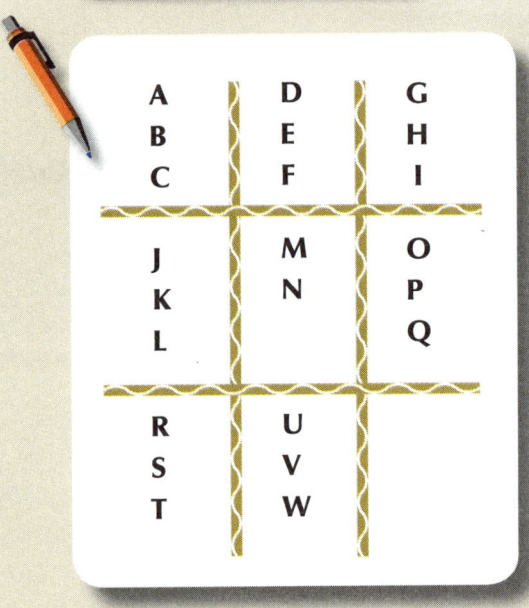

A	D	G
B	E	H
C	F	I
J	M	O
K	N	P
L		Q
R	U	
S	V	
T	W	

Use the code to find places where you can pray to God. Find the shape in the grid.
The placement of the dot in the shape (top, center, or bottom) tells what letter to write in the blank.

1. I can pray in a _ _ _ _ _ _

Praying in ___ ___ ___ ___ ___ ___ is good

because _____

2. I can pray in my _ _ _ _ ___ ___ ___ ___. This is a good

place to pray because _____

3. I can pray _ _ _ _ _ _ _ _

___ ___ ___ ___ ___ ___ ___ ___. This is a good place to pray because

_____

26

Friendship with God

I Believe

Write yes next to each statement you believe.

_____ Family members need love.　　_____ Pollution can affect a person's health.

_____ The Earth revolves around the sun.　　_____ I am a child of God.

> **The word *creed* comes from *credo*, a Latin word that means "I believe." A creed says what we believe. Catholics have two creeds. The Apostles' Creed is a summary of the faith of the apostles. It is often the first creed young Catholics learn.**

The creed we usually proclaim at Mass on Sunday comes from a meeting called the Council of Nicaea. In 325, bishops of the Church met in the city of Nicaea. They agreed on a way to state the beliefs of the Church. This statement of beliefs is called the Nicene Creed. The city of Nicaea no longer exists, but the Nicene Creed does. During Mass, Catholics stand and tell what they believe by proclaiming the Nicene Creed.

This Is What We Believe

The Nicene Creed is made up of three parts, one for each person of the Holy Trinity. Read each clue. If the clue is a belief about God the Father, write an F in the blank. Write a J if the belief is about Jesus, and write HS if it is about the Holy Spirit.

★ maker of heaven and earth _____

★ born of the Virgin Mary, and became man _____

★ With the Father and the Son he is worshiped and glorified _____

★ the Father, the Almighty _____

★ he suffered, died, and was buried. On the third day he rose again _____

★ the giver of life _____

★ He will come again in glory to judge the living and the dead _____

★ maker ... of all that is seen and unseen _____

★ the only Son of God _____

★ he ascended into heaven _____

And that's a fact...

Saint Nicholas was born in the part of the world now known as Turkey. Because there are many stories about Nicholas that show him helping young people, he is the model for Santa Claus. But Nicholas was also Bishop of Myra, one of the bishops who attended the Council of Nicaea in 325, and helped create the Nicene Creed.

I Pray

The Prayer of the Church

When the apostles asked Jesus to teach them to pray, he taught them the prayer we call the Our Father, or the Lord's Prayer. Because this prayer uses Jesus' words, it is prayed at every celebration of the Eucharist. The prayer is also said at Baptisms and Confirmations.

The Lord's Prayer is the prayer of the Church. When you pray the Our Father, you're united with God's Family, past and present.

What Am I Saying?

When you pray the Lord's Prayer, you say the same words Jesus said 2,000 years ago! These questions and answers can help you to understand this important prayer.

The first lines praise God.

Our Father, who art in heaven,	What does the name *Father* tell you about God? The word *heaven* describes eternal life with God.
hallowed be thy name;	*Hallowed* means "holy." How should God's name be used?
thy kingdom come;	*Thy* means "your." We are reminded to follow Jesus.
thy will be done on earth as it is in heaven.	We promise to live as God wants us to so Earth can become more like heaven. That definitely includes meeting the needs of others. What is one way you do as God wants?

The next four lines are requests.

Give us this day our daily bread;	The word *bread* is used to mean "what we need in life." What do you need in order to serve God?
and forgive us our trespasses as we forgive those who trespass against us;	*Trespasses* mean "sins." What does this request mean to you? Think of instances in your life that call for you to forgive in the same way that someone forgave you.
and lead us not into temptation,	Name two temptations that fifth graders face.
but deliver us from evil.	What is one evil in the world?
Amen.	*Amen* means "I believe" or "This is true."

Friendship with God

Why Do We Pray?

Friends and families stay close by talking often. They share news and support one another. They ask for help. And when they have hurt one another, they ask for forgiveness.

People pray to God for the same reasons they talk with others.
- **People praise God.**
- **People tell God they're sorry for things they've done wrong, and they ask forgiveness.**
- **People ask for help with prayers of petition.**
- **People give God thanks.**

Your relationship with God depends on good, frequent communication. Prayer is like the food that feeds your friendship with him.

A Special Gift

Think of someone you care about. Get ready to give that person the gift of prayer. Pray for the person every day for one month.

- Spend a few quiet moments thinking about the person you chose.
- Use the suggestions below to write your prayer.
- Decorate the prayer with signs that tell about the person.
- Pray the prayer today and every day for a month.

Dear God,

You are (Use words of praise for God.) _____.

Thank you for (Write the person's name.) _____

who is (Write words of praise that describe the person.) _____

_____.

I ask you, God, to bless (Write the person's name.) _____

with (Write words that describe what good things you are asking for the person.) _____

_____.

For this I pray, Amen.

I Pray

I Respond to God's Love

When your dad helps you feel better, how do you respond?
_____

When your mom hugs you, how do you respond?
_____

When your friend cheers for you during your soccer game, how do you respond?
_____

When your teacher says your report was very good, how do you respond?
_____

Praising and Thanking God

Prayer is your response to the love God gives you.
- When you see a beautiful tree, what can you say to God?
- At the end of the day, what can you say to God?
- Before you eat, what can you say to God?
- When someone is kind to you, what can you say to God?

Asking Prayers

In addition to thanking and praising God, people often ask God for help. When asking God for something, a person needs to know who God is.

Some people think of God as a kind of Santa Claus. They expect God to give them whatever they want. Let's say that you didn't study for your social studies test. Your Santa Claus prayer might be: Dear God, please help me pass this test.

A person who believes in God's grace and in the power of the Holy Spirit might pray: Dear Holy Spirit, guide me in my studying. Let my mind be focused. If there's something I don't understand, let me ask for help. Be with me as I take the test.

God is love. When you ask God for something, let your prayer be a response to God's love. Ask to be more loving like God.

Imagine that you and your sister fight every day. Circle the prayer that responds to God's love.

God, make my sister stop fighting.

God, you made me a smart person. Help me figure out a way to get along with my sister.

Friendship with God

The Church Responds to God's Love

Do you ever see people showing their love in public ways? Circle the public signs of affection in the sentences below.

- Jan gave her daughter, Lucy, a hug after Lucy's piano recital.
- When Jose walked down the jet way, he could see his parents' sign:
- "Welcome home, Jose!"
- Grandma and Grandpa held hands as they walked through the garden.

> The Family of God responds to God's love with private prayer and with public prayer.
>
> Public praise and honor given to God is called worship. Liturgy is the public worship of the Church. In the liturgy worshipers pray all together. They celebrate God's love. As one people, they offer prayers to God in the name of Jesus through the Holy Spirit.

Wall Art

The Church community publicly worships God in the sacraments. The Eucharist is the Church's greatest act of worship.

On the church wall, draw a mural that shows the Family of God worshiping publicly.

31

A Year in the Church

I Pray

> Throughout the year, the Church celebrates seasons and feasts. Because the celebrations are liturgies, the Church calendar is called the liturgical year.

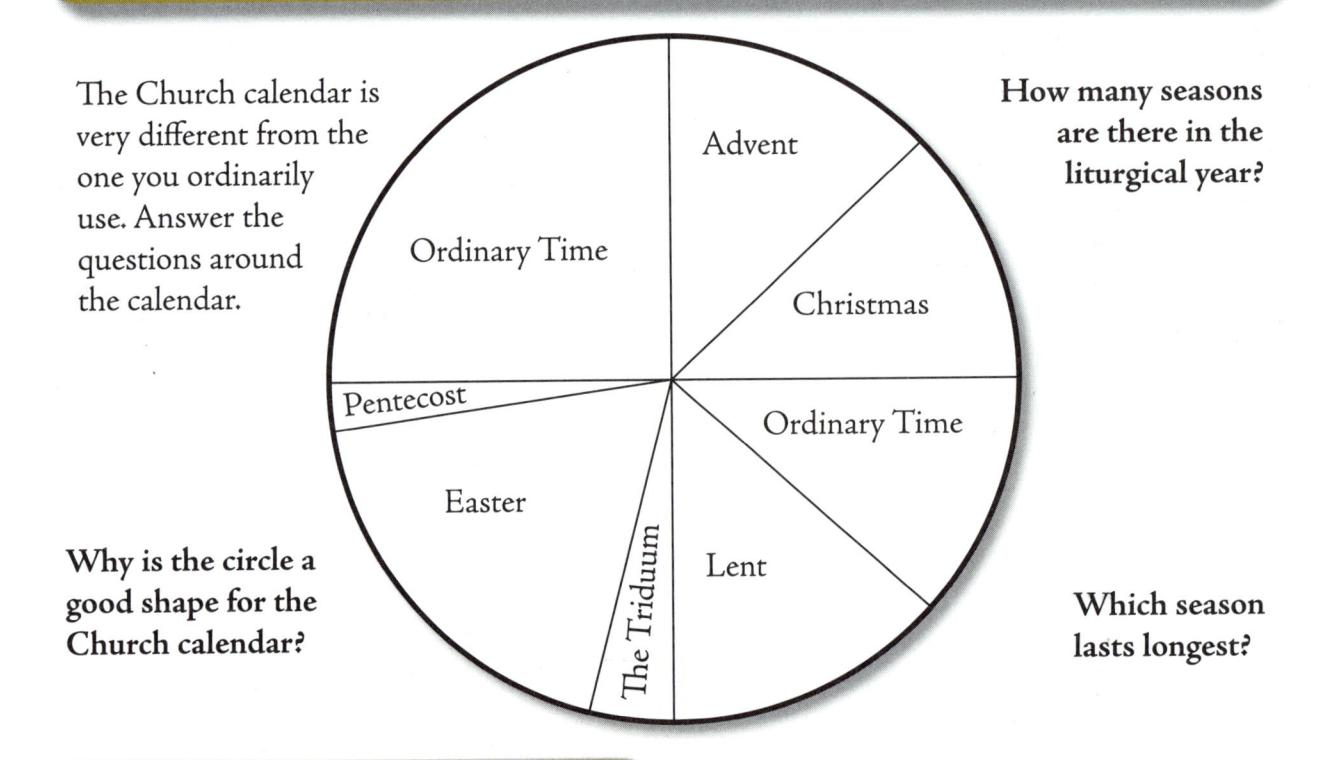

The Church calendar is very different from the one you ordinarily use. Answer the questions around the calendar.

Calendar wheel sections: Advent, Christmas, Ordinary Time, Lent, The Triduum, Easter, Pentecost, Ordinary Time

How many seasons are there in the liturgical year?

Why is the circle a good shape for the Church calendar?

Which season lasts longest?

Complete the Calendar

Each season in the Church year recalls an event in Jesus' life—his birth, life, death, resurrection, and ascension. Each season is marked with a color. The priest's vestments, the altar cloth, and church decorations all use that color. The liturgical calendar on this page is missing its colors. Fill them in, using the clues.

Violet—The Church year begins. People prepare for the coming of Jesus.

White or gold—The Church celebrates Jesus' birth, his Holy Family, and his Baptism.

Violet—The Church remembers Jesus' suffering and death.

White or gold—The Church celebrates Jesus' resurrection.

Green—This season is celebrated in two parts. The Church celebrates Mary and the feasts of many other saints. People grow in the understanding of their faith.

Red—On Good Friday, the Church remembers the day Jesus died.

White or gold—On Holy Thursday, the Church remembers the day that Jesus gave us the Eucharist.

White or gold—On Holy Saturday, the Church waits and watches for the resurrection of Jesus.

Red—The Church celebrates Pentecost, the coming of the Holy Spirit.